Marriage in a Nutshell

Proverbs About Marriage
Selected with Commentaries From
The Biblical Book of Proverbs
And Other Sources

Robert Harris

.: Virtual**Salt**
Publishing
Tustin

Marriage in a Nutshell
Proverbs about Marriage Selected with Commentaries from the Biblical Book of Proverbs and Other Sources

VirtualSalt Publishing, Tustin, California
© 2014 Robert Harris
All rights reserved

ISBN 978-1-941233-06-1

www.virtualsalt.com

Cover image by Bartek Ambrozik

Introduction

Ask not what your marriage can do for you;
Ask what you can do for your marriage.

I was recently thinking about the elaborate, time-consuming thought and planning that go into preparing for a wedding: months of identifying and evaluating alternatives, weighing criteria, making and refining choices, seeking input from friends and experts alike. No wonder the engaged couple reaches decision fatigue. Truly, preparing for a wedding is an elaborate undertaking.

Then it occurred to me: How much time and effort are spent preparing for the marriage itself? Perhaps a few hours of premarital counseling? Or maybe only sharing the results of a magazine "compatibility test"? Wouldn't it be great if couples would spend as much time preparing to be married as they do preparing for the wedding? Wouldn't that make the "big adjustment" a lot easier, or even nonexistent? Frankly, wouldn't it be nice if couples knew a bit more about what they are getting into?

That's why I put this little book together. The book is a collection of proverbs, Biblical and others, that speak to the married life and offer some teaching about how to build a Christian marriage and how to make that life more fulfilling. There are many helpful books about marriage, interpersonal relationships, understanding how men and women differ, and how to flourish in a marriage, but many couples don't have the time or inclination to go through those books. What they need is the condensed summary, presented in little, easily digestible snippets that can be chewed on during spare moments. What they need is marriage in a nutshell.

That's this book.

One last note: You will notice that I occasionally cover the same topic more than once—okay, I repeat myself. But that's mainly because the topic I'm discussing again bears repeating. And as for the multiple entries about contentious wives, those stem from the repetition of the idea in the Proverbs themselves. (I've tried to include all of the Biblical proverbs from Proverbs that address marriage.)

Now, thanks to my best friend, inspiration, and excellent wife (Proverbs 31:10), Marie, for her encouragement with this project.

Tustin, January 2014

Part One
Biblical Proverbs

Do not let kindness and truth leave you;
Bind them around your neck,
Write them on the tablet of your heart,
So you will find favor and good repute
In the sight of God and man.
—Proverbs 3:3-4

It might seem like a strange pair, but two critically important characteristics for building and maintaining a relationship are kindness and truth.

Kindness can be a few words of appreciation, love, or support, or it can be a simple caress, a note, a backrub, or even a small gift. It's the emotional accompaniment to whatever you say or do that is important.

Truth means honesty in the relationship. It doesn't mean criticizing your spouse in the name of truth ("You seem to be gaining a lot of weight; better lay off those chocolates"). It does mean admitting that you lost the TV remote or that you give an honest answer when asked if you enjoy, say, going fishing.

Drink water from your own cistern,
And fresh water from your own well.
And rejoice in the wife of your youth.
—Proverbs 5:15, 18a

Be faithful to your own wife and don't commit adultery (drinking water from your neighbor's cistern). And don't just put up with, don't just endure, don't just live with, but rejoice in your wife. If that seems difficult or impossible, work on your relationship. Spend time together, talking, making something, serving others.

It has been known since the days of Aristotle that if you act in a certain way, your beliefs and feelings will eventually harmonize with those actions. So, if you are feeling cold or bored or frustrated with your spouse, act as if you were feeling warm, interested, and happy with your spouse. You will be surprised at the difference. And your spouse just might change, too, since changing yourself is always the first step toward an improved spouse.

Hatred stirs up strife,
But love covers all transgressions.
— Proverbs 10:12

Exchanging negative, critical, unloving com-ments only perpetuates the strife and ten-sion and coldness in a marriage. Showing real love, consideration, understanding, forgiveness, and kindness will wash away the faults and hurts. It's a choice. Which behavior do you think will make your spouse happier? Which do you think will make you happier?

Love, real love, has a strange way of cover-ing transgressions. First, the saying, "Love is blind," means that in a marriage partnership, spouses simply don't see the "transgressions" that other people see. To use our standard ex-ample, a loving partner who sees the cap miss-ing from the toothpaste tube simply doesn't see that fact as a transgression on the spouse's part. The partner simply puts the cap back on and moves on to the mouthwash or whatever is the next item on the day's agenda.

Second, the spouse might recognize a fail-ing in the partner, but just doesn't care. In the context of the relationship, the spouse allows the partner to be human and to possess individual quirks.

Andrea: Why, Paula, I never saw such a germophobic man as your husband. He even washes the doorknobs.

Paula: Yeah, he keeps things clean all right.

Andrea: Doesn't that bug you?

Paula: Not at all. I know it might seem a bit excessive, but on the other hand, we've not had colds for three years.

Third, the spouse might be bothered by the partner's behavior, but simply accepts it out of love and doesn't say anything.

Bill: Hey, Sid. I've noticed that your wife interrupts you and talks over you.

Sid: Yeah, she does.

Bill: Doesn't that bother you? I'd be fuming.

Sid: It bothers me some, sure. But I've decided not to say anything.

Bill: Why ever not?

Sid: It's her long standing habit, and I doubt she could change it. And besides, it's too minor an irritation to bring up right now.

A gracious woman attains honor.
— Proverbs 11:16a

Yes, the gracious — the kind, pleasant, amiable — woman is just more fun to be around, and gains the high reputation she deserves. She is honored for her easygoing personality, and her willingness to jump in and help cheerfully.

Maybe this is the place to mention that Secret Key #1 to a Successful and Happy Marriage is to focus your relational energies, choices, habits, practices — and words — on making life for your spouse easier rather than more difficult.

That's why, when coming home from work and turning the corner onto his street, the husband of a gracious wife starts to relax and to become aware of a feeling of comfort and anticipation rising in his heart. As he pulls into his driveway, he says to himself, "Ah, home at last to my sanctuary and my loving wife, the delight of my life."

As a ring of gold in a swine's snout,
So is a beautiful woman who lacks discretion.
—Proverbs 11:22

The point of this proverb is to remind us that discretion—being careful and considerate in one's speech and actions—is more important than looks for a lastingly happy marriage. True, gorgeous women who are wise and circumspect are wonderful, but discretion, like amiability and compassion and good sense, makes a woman attractive in a way that even very good looks by themselves just can't match.

This proverb also reminds wives not to gossip, especially about their husbands.

An excellent wife is the crown of her husband,
But she who shames him
Is as rottenness to his bones.
—Proverbs 12:4

An excellent wife makes her husband so happy that he feels like a king. Of all the possessions, talents, friends, and power he may have, his excellent wife is his crown, his glory that establishes his heart in joy. She is the earthly relationship that empowers him and makes him feel like royalty.

And since, as the saying is, the corruption of the best of things creates the worst of things, so is a wife who brings shame on her husband. Having rotten bones isn't a good thing; feeling *as if* you have rotten bones can't be much better.

There is one who speaks rashly
Like the thrusts of a sword,
But the tongue of the wise brings healing.
— Proverbs 12:18

Too many people do not realize what a powerful instrument the tongue is. A harsh word can do a lot of damage, while a kind word can heal deep hurts.

The saying, "Sticks and stones will break my bones, but words can never hurt me," is false. The truth is, "A stick hurts for an hour, but words can hurt for years."

"Think before you speak" has become almost a cliché, but there is good reason for it. Unfortunately, this advice is sometimes ignored.

When you are tempted to say something critical to your spouse, especially if you are going to add a harsh tone of voice, first ask yourself, "What do I expect the result to be? Will my comment make my spouse happier? If not, why should I say it? Or do I think it will make me happier? Do I really think that making my spouse unhappy will make me happy?"

And if you fire a verbal salvo at your spouse, what will your spouse do? Do you think the next ten minutes will be a time of strengthening your relationship and increasing your marital satisfaction?

It is unfortunate that when some spouses disagree, one spouse or both will make comments intended to hurt the other one. This use of words as punishment is what some parents do with their children, when the parent wants the child to know "how much his actions bother me."

But, Get a Clue #1: Your spouse is not your child. Don't treat your life partner the way you treat your kids. It's condescending and humiliating and devaluing. So just stop it.

(And Parental Hint #1: You shouldn't treat your kids this way, either. Verbal beatings are very harmful to children as well as adults.)

Use your tongue to soothe and heal, not to stab and cut.

The wise woman builds her house,
But the foolish tears it down
With her own hands.
— Proverbs 14:1

Marriage is a house you build together with your spouse. The wise woman builds her house by building up her husband. Words of appreciation and support toward her husband help him grow stronger and more confident — and more loving toward his wife. The foolish woman uses criticism and complaint and lecturing to punish her husband. Emotionally destructive words tear him down and the house is torn apart.

Marriages succeed and are continuously built up through kindness and compassion, or fail by being constantly torn apart through bickering and disapproval — by either spouse, or both.

External threats and attacks can be repelled by a strong marriage partnership, heavily influenced by the wisdom of the wife; but internal strife can be fatal, especially when the partners act foolishly and inconsiderately.

Before you engage in the next altercation, stop and ask yourself, "Why am I planning to use these words, these details, and this tone of voice? Am I confident that they will make my spouse happier and my marriage stronger? Or will they rip out yet another supporting beam, one less to hold the roof up?"

Note finally, this proverb focuses on the wise and foolish women because women wield the greater emotional power in a marriage. Men deeply need respect, approval, and encouragement, and the wives who provide that build their houses on solid ground. And in such a house dwells a husband's love.

A gentle answer turns away wrath,
But a harsh word stirs up anger.
— Proverbs 15:1

Respond to anger by listening and seeking to understand sympathetically. Letting your spouse vent will enable him or her to feel heard. Lack of push back or resistance will calm your partner down. On the other hand, if you object, contradict, or resist, you will only make the anger worse, because it will appear to your spouse that you are invalidating his or her feelings and issue.

When your spouse lashes out at you in anger, you might be tempted to pick up your verbal weapons and do battle, with the result that the argument will escalate until perhaps you are breaking grandma's fine china.

On the other hand, if you respond gently, you might surprise your spouse, and soon calm the waters. A one-sided rant soon makes the arguer feel a bit foolish.

And something that we all know but that many of us seldom practice often enough is the fact that apologies are free. If your spouse lashes out at you, why not gently and warmly and sincerely say you are sorry? If you don't feel that you have done anything wrong, at least say you're sorry that your spouse is upset.

Some people lose their ability to think rationally when they are angry. And raging irrationality is not a pretty sight. If this is you, next time you feel anger welling up against your spouse, stop the discussion, tell your spouse that you need to take a break to calm down, and go on a walk by yourself for a while. Later, when you can discuss the issue calmly, get together again.

Even serious disagreements — no, make that *especially* serious disagreements — ought to be handled respectfully and reasonably.

Here's a thought: Imagine that your dispute is going to be recorded for a reality TV show called "Spousal Spats." The whole argument will be broadcast to the world. Yes, your mom, grandma, the kids, the neighbors, curious strangers by the million — they will all see it. Let that thought guide your interaction.

A soothing tongue is a tree of life,
But perversion in it crushes the spirit.
—Proverbs 15:4

You have no doubt noticed how many of these Biblical proverbs involve the power of talking. That's because words have impact.

Ask yourself, of all the words you speak to your spouse in a day or a week, what percentage are positive, complimentary, uplifting, supportive words and what percentage are negative, critical, contentious, contradicting words?

Next question: Would you say you are interested in energizing your marriage or are you interested in crushing its spirit?

Logic problem. See if you can understand these two formulas:

Happy Wife = Happy Husband
Happy Husband = Happy Wife

Final Exam: True or False. You can make yourself happier and more fulfilled by making your spouse miserable.

Better is a dish of vegetables where love is,
Than a fattened ox and hatred with it.
—Proverbs 15:17

Marriage is only slightly about money, food, possessions, sex, and children. It's mostly about living a cooperative adventure.

The real power and value in marriage is the emotional and spiritual bond between husband and wife that makes this cooperative adventure possible, and even enjoyable. Marriage is about an emotional relationship, a psychic partnership, a team of two friends who have each other's back.

That's why this proverb tells us that vegetables served with a side order of love beats steak with a side order of hatred any day of the week.

See also Proverbs 15:16.

Pride goes before destruction,
And a haughty spirit before stumbling.
—Proverbs 16:18

What does this proverb have to do with marriage, you may ask? Well, a major problem with some couples is that they can't get out from under their own egos so that they can simply enjoy their spouse and their marriage.

Want to have a happy marriage? Humble yourself, stop trying to control your spouse or to make your spouse into someone exactly like you. Instead, serve your spouse's needs.

Just as life in general is not about you, so marriage is not about you, either. Marriage is not a relationship you enter merely for what you can get out of it. Relationships are built through mutual sacrifice and service, with both partners kicking pride off the throne.

To paraphrase President Kennedy, "Ask not what your marriage can do for you; ask what you can do for your marriage."

Bright eyes gladden the heart.
— Proverbs 15:30a

This proverb is a reminder that when you and your spouse meet again after being separated by the workday or any other reason, you should make an effort to put on your happy face and cheerful tone, reflecting the joy of reunion, and showing that you are glad to meet again.

In every reunion, the first 30 seconds are crucial. Your husband or wife will lock in what appears to be your mood and will interpret your subsequent comments and actions by that initial appearance.

Greeting your spouse with bright eyes sets the right tone. And adding a meaningful hug or kiss couldn't hurt, either.

Pleasant words are a honeycomb,
Sweet to the soul and healing to the bones.
—Proverbs 16:24

Successful marriage is an emotional partnership. Kind words, encouragement, and support are the glue that holds the marriage together. Think of marriage as a friendship taken to the next level.

Supporting words = Stronger relationship
Kind words = Contentment
Complimentary words = Courage
Encouraging words = Confidence
Forgiving words = Healing
Reassuring words = Security

Pleasant words do more to make a marriage happy than any other thing.

Oh, and don't forget a warm tone of voice.

Better is a dry morsel and quietness with it
Than a house full of feasting with strife.
—Proverbs 17:1

The home should be a sanctuary where husband and wife can join together in peace and security, safe from the tensions and stresses of the day.

Home should be a place of mutual support, an alliance, not a combat zone.

All of us need a place and a friend where together we can "let our hair down," relax, decompress, and regain our sanity and our sense of self—including our sense of self worth.

When the house is not a place to exhale and relax the tense muscles—when the opposite of a sanctuary is present—the feelings of tension and strife grow larger, and the entire person grows weaker, as does the relationship itself.

Save that attitude of "crush the competition" for the boardroom or tennis court. Don't bring it home with you.

The contentions of a wife
Are a constant dripping.
—Proverbs 19:13b

If the book of Proverbs had been written by a woman, this proverb would probably say something like, "The stubbornness of a man is like an ox stuck in the mud." The difference tells us about men and women.

A man with a contentious wife feels rejected and incompetent because she seems to him to imply that he is always wrong. A woman with a stubborn husband feels devalued because he seems to her to refuse to validate her feelings and needs.

You can see that each one's behavior reinforces the other's behavior.

Remedy: Wives, stop trying to fix, change, or improve your husbands, especially by nagging. Husbands, listen to your wives and allow yourselves to be influenced by them.

He who finds a wife finds a good thing,
And obtains favor from the LORD.
—Proverbs 18:22

In a loving, Biblical marriage, a wife truly is a blessing from the Lord, a blessing that continues to grow and deepen and enrich as time goes on.

Like any other "good thing," however, this blessing requires care and maintenance. If the blessing were a car, men would understand this, paying close attention to its needs, buying it toys, and bragging about it. They know that the better the maintenance, the more reliable the car. Neglect paying attention to service, and your car just might let you down.

So, husbands, keep your wife a "good thing," by providing the care she needs. Listen when she needs to talk, be considerate of her needs, reassure her regularly that you love her and that you care about her happiness.

Give her some flowers on an ordinary day for no special reason at all—other than that you love her.

What is desirable in a man is his kindness.
— Proverbs 19:22a

If I had to guess, I'd say this is the proverb that wives will pick out as their favorite among the others quoted in this book.

Husbands, what's the deal here? Can you be a little more effortful and deliberate in showing kindness to your wives? A little softer, not so gruff, not so demanding? And how about consulting her more often when you face those larger decisions? Remember, she's your partner.

Being head of the household doesn't give you license to be controlling, bossy, or commandeering, much less mean and cruel.

So, how about lightening up? How about being thoughtful and generous (bought her any earrings lately?), or as the proverb says, being kind?

And, for heaven's sake, can you pick up your socks and underwear and put the toilet seat down?

It is better to live in a desert land,
Than with a contentious and vexing woman.
— Proverbs 21:19

In order to understand why the book of Proverbs contains a number of similar sayings about contentious and vexing wives, several factors need to be taken into consideration.

First, men are much more sensitive, with their fragile eggshell egos, than their wives probably believe is possible for such supposedly rugged men. But the truth is, criticism and conflict from one's hoped-for ally and supporter can hurt a man deeply.

Second, wives who vex their husbands by constantly arguing with them might not intend to send the message of rejection and disrespect that their husbands are receiving. If you're in doubt about how your husband perceives you, try this. At some opportune moment in a casual conversation, say, "I agree completely." Your husband's reaction will tell you everything you need to know. If you can't find an opportune moment to say those words, that will also tell you something. (If you say them and like the reaction, use them regularly, together with the other Magic Words. See page 93.)

Men have a profound need to feel competent and, just like women, a need to feel validated. Contentiousness prevents these feelings from growing and blossoming in a man's heart.

The takeaway from the above is that poor communication—poor understanding of the intended message—is perhaps the largest cause of marital disharmony, argument, hurt, confusion, and unhappiness.

Wives can be less contentious and less vexing by

> ✠ Looking for points of agreement rather than disagreement.
>
> ✠ Reassuring their husbands that the comments are in the context of love and respect.

Husbands can help their wives to avoid contentiousness and vexing by

> ✠ Responding to their wives' legitimate complaints.
>
> ✠ Attending to "honey, do" requests in a timely way.

A man's pride will bring him low,
But a humble spirit will obtain honor.
—Proverbs 29:23

Someday I'm going to write an entire book about pride and its horrible consequences. It will be a long, ugly book because pride is the source of a phenomenal amount of pain and heartache—needless pain and heartache. This is sadly true in some marriages, too.

Remember Jesus' teaching: "Whoever wishes to become great among you shall be your servant" (Matthew 20:26b). And Paul applies this to everyday relationships, including marriage partners: "Be willing to serve each other out of respect for Christ" (Ephesians 5:21, ERV).

So, next time you are irritated at your spouse for a horrible crime such as chipping a dish or neglecting to put the soda back in the refrigerator, get down off your high horse and think about how blessed you are that someone would actually marry you, of all people, and go give your spouse a loving hug of gratitude.

House and wealth
Are an inheritance from fathers,
But a prudent wife is from the LORD.
—Proverbs 19:14

Prudence, also called wisdom, was one of the four classical virtues (prudence, temperance, justice, and fortitude). A prudent wife exercises self-discipline toward her own desires, good stewardship in the use of resources, and wise judgment in general.

Husbands of women like this rejoice in their wives' circumspection, reasonableness, and practicality.

Truly, such a wife is from the Lord, a wonderful gift who smooths the road and calms the waters.

It is better to live in a corner of the roof
Than in a house
Shared with a contentious woman.
—Proverbs 25:24

Wives who are always on their husbands about something make their husbands feel incompetent, unloved, rejected, insecure, unwanted, controlled, untrusted, and mothered. The husbands conclude that such wives now believe that their husbands are not good enough for them and regret marrying them.

Sometimes, contention in a marriage is the result of a power struggle. Before marriage, the couple did not decide who will wear the pants in the family or how the marriage will be managed. As a result, after marriage, instead of building a partnership, the couple become competitors and engage in a struggle for dominance and control.

Spouses in these marriages engage in an overt and forceful insistence on their rights, their opinions, their way of doing things, and their own standards. When one spouse doesn't follow the other's rules, a fight ensues.

Suggestions for remedying this issue:

1. Realize that you and your spouse are different people with different standards and values and tastes.

2. Realize that men and women think differently and feel differently. Assuming that your spouse has the same perceptions and reactions as you do can cause plenty of misunderstanding.

3. Agree with your spouse that building and maintaining a loving relationship is more important than (a) putting the cap back on the toothpaste tube, (b) identifying who actually left the cap off, or (c) proceeding to discuss (a) and (b) at length.

4. Read Ephesians, Chapter 5 together and discuss it.

An angry man stirs up strife,
And a hot-tempered man
Abounds in transgression.
—Proverbs 29:22

It's one thing to be angry, but another to act it out. Acting out anger is a choice, as anyone knows who has been in the middle of a blazing argument when the phone rings. The red-faced screamer suddenly becomes calm and polite to the caller.

So, point number one: No matter how angry you are, remain calm and polite and don't act out your emotions. Let your reason prevail and discuss the issue rationally, without hurtful tones of voice or nasty comments.

Point number two, for men especially. Your wife knows that you are probably much stronger than she is physically, and anger and violence are associated (who would have guessed?). So when you start fuming, your wife can easily become very frightened, fearful that you might hurt her. Is it worth making the woman who loves you feel afraid of being harmed, just so you can externalize your feelings?

Point three. Angry arguments tend to escalate, as one partner sends a missile one way and the other partner sends a slightly larger one back. This continues until nuclear war happens, unless something breaks the pattern.

(A great example of how the escalation can be broken comes from one wife, who, when she sensed the argument was going out of control, would suddenly stick out her tongue at her husband, causing them both to start laughing. This action allowed a time out in the argument that allowed emotions to cool and reason to take over.)

Point four. Some people say really stupid things when they are raging at their spouse, things they really don't mean but things that cause hurt that will be remembered for a long time. Even if your spouse knows that what you said was preposterous, he or she will remember that the reason you said it was to cause emotional hurt. Expressing regret, repentance, and apology will help some, but the memory remains.

If you are prone to angry insults, memorize a few proverbs that can remind you to think before you speak:

> ✠ You can't unfry an egg.
> ✠ You can't unthrow a dart.
> ✠ You can't unshoot an arrow.

A constant dripping on a day of steady rain
And a contentious woman are alike.
—Proverbs 27:15

The problem of contentiousness has been discussed already. But the analogy in this proverb bears a brief comment.

Once a husband gets the idea that he needs to attend to something, he's usually good to go. If his wife continues to discuss the situation after he has agreed to handle it, he feels demeaned, devalued, and humiliated, because the "lecture" his wife is giving him feels like punishment—like torture from a constant dripping.

Now, the wife might not intend her words to be received this way because she is just exploring her feelings and thinking about the issue. Or she might think she is helping her husband with her comments, supplying context and details. But, and this is a difference in male and female temperaments, that's not the message the husband receives.

Note how Tom misinterprets Jane's comments in the following scenario:

Jane: Tom, the downstairs toilet keeps leaking.
Could you take a look at it?

Tom: Sure, darling, right after dinner.

Jane: It's important not to have a leak in the toilet because that can waste a lot of water and raise our water bills. And we also want to remember that water is an increasingly scarce resource. It's good environmentally to be sure that water isn't wasted by leaks. The water bill always has an insert about saving precious water and saying that leaks, especially in toilets, are a main cause of water waste in homes. Our water bill last month was $61. I wonder how much of that was due to the toilet leak?

Tom (angrily): I said I'd fix it after dinner. What do you want from me, anyway?

Sometimes, husbands think their wives are being contentious and expressing doubt about the husband's competence when the wife is simply asking questions to learn more. Example:

Sam: I'm going to ask Frank for a promotion.

Sally: Do you think you qualify?

Sam (irritated): Yes, why do you doubt me?

Sally: I don't doubt you. I just wondered what you have accomplished that merits a promotion.

Sam (blowing his cool): You have no idea how much work I put in at the office.

Sally (starting to get upset at Sam's tone): You're right, I don't. You don't talk much about what you do. How am I supposed to know?

An excellent wife, who can find?
For her worth is far above jewels.
The heart of her husband trusts in her,
And he will have no lack of gain.
She does him good and not evil
All the days of her life.
—Proverbs 31:10-12

Those familiar with the Bible will recognize Proverbs 31:10-31 as a key descriptor of an excellent wife. In these verses we find that the excellent wife is trustworthy (11), moral (12), happy and content (13b), energetic (15a), intelligent (16a), healthy (17), hardworking (18b), generous and compassionate (20), brave (21a), skilled (22), enterprising (24), wise (26a), kind (26b), active (27), and faithful to God (30b).

Of all these attributes, being faithful to God is, of course, the most important, but hard on its heels is the first one, trust. Every relationship stands or falls depending on the level of trust in it. If you cannot trust your spouse, you don't have a real relationship. You might have a transactional arrangement—you do this and I'll do that—but not a relationship. The more trust you have, the stronger your relationship will be.

Trust is the foundation of confidence, safety, security, and comfortableness in a relationship. If you want a good relationship, work to build trust and don't do anything that will reduce it. Be a brick, as they say in England — a solid, reliable partner who can be counted on.

Watch over your heart with all diligence,
For from it flow the springs of life.
—Proverbs 4:23

When young people want to decide on whom to date once, an important reason is often, "Well, she's beautiful," or, "Well, he's cute."

When they want to go steady, the reason changes to, "Well, she has a fun personality," or, "Well, he's funny and interesting."

But when they want to get married, the reason for their choice focuses on, "Well, she is such a good hearted girl," or, "Well, he has a kind heart."

Hence this proverb about keeping an eye on your heart. Watching over your heart means not only keeping it safe from foolish, indulgent whims, but taking care to nurture it in such a way that it can indeed become the source of the springs of life for those you meet only once, for those you become friends with, and for the person you marry.

Put away from you a deceitful mouth,
And put devious lips far from you.
—Proverbs 4:24

Every relationship—whether it's of friend-ship, coworker, business to business, or marriage—begins with a token amount of trust given by each side to the other. After that, trust is gained slowly by earning it, by demonstrating that the partner in the relationship is trust-worthy.

Unfortunately, there is so much untrustwor-thiness in modern life that trust itself has be-come tentative much longer than it used to be. Moreover, it is more fragile than ever before.

Hence this proverb applies powerfully to marriage. Lies and deceit can cause severe damage to a relationship—damage that can take longer to repair than you might imagine. In the area of deceit, once we find out that our trusted partner has lied or deceived even one time, we naturally wonder how many other times we have been fooled.

Think about the following scenario. Nor-man, afraid of getting into an argument if he were to be honest, chooses a simple lie.

Norman and his coworker Kristin were working on the Simpkins account together when lunch time arrived. So that they would not lose momentum, and still have the opportunity to get away from the office, they decided to go to lunch at a local grill.

That evening, when Norman got home, his wife asked him what he did for lunch that day. Not wanting to cause his wife any jealous feelings, he decided on a convenient deception and said, "Tom and I went to lunch at a nearby coffee shop."

Unfortunately, an acquaintance of Norman and his wife had seen Norman at the grill with "another woman" and had called Norman's wife that day. Now, no matter how much apologizing, explaining, and back pedaling Norman does, his wife's trust in him has been damaged.

When there are many words,
Transgression is unavoidable,
But he who restrains his lips is wise.
—Proverbs 10:19

I know what you're thinking. You think I'm going to use this as advice to women not to talk so much. You are wrong.

Women talk to see what they think and to understand how they feel. Talk is therapy for them. But when they explore their feelings and frustrations with their husbands as the audience, the husband often wants to jump in and solve the problem by giving unwanted advice.

The fact is, when a woman actually wants advice, she uses the same secret code phrase men do when they want advice: "What do you think I should do?"

So the proverb tells us not only to "Think before you speak," but for husbands to listen attentively—and quietly—when their wives are venting.

Also: Proverbs 13:3, 17:27, 21:23, and 29:20.

Commit your works to the LORD
And your plans will be established.
—Proverbs 16:3

This final entry from the book of Proverbs reminds us that putting God at the center of your marriage and seeking his will and guidance will provide the foundation and operational wisdom for a solid, satisfying marriage.

Seek God prayerfully in every decision, and commit the efforts of your marital partnership—your team—to his service (and not, by the way, to the individual self-indulgence of either of you), and your marriage will be blessed.

Nevertheless let each individual among you
Also love his own wife even as himself;
And let the wife see to it that she
Respect her husband.
—Ephesians 5:33

Of all the verses in the Bible on marriage outside of the book of Proverbs, this one encapsulates the path to marital happiness more completely than any other. Rightly under-stood and rightly applied, this Scripture would bring happiness and contentment to a large percentage of troubled marriages.

Husbands, love your wives. Love is singled out in this Scripture for men to give to their wives in part because wives need regular, or even frequent, reassurance that they are loved. Let them know that you care about them. Listen to them when they need to talk (and don't offer solutions, just listen). Show your wife some af-fection. Tell her you appreciate her. Tell her that you are glad you married her.

Wives, respect your husbands. Respect is singled out in this Scripture for wives to give to their husbands because disrespect is the most hurtful and damaging attitude a wife can dis-play toward her husband. Never roll your eyes in contempt, don't criticize, don't correct your husband publicly. When you disagree, put your disagreement in the form of a question. That is, instead of saying, "You're wrong. It was Joe Green who said that, not Ted Brown," ask, "Wasn't it Joe Green who said that?" or "Ted Brown? I thought it was Joe Green."

Here's how.

Husbands: Love involves communicating with your wife, and making her feel secure and safe. Get to know your wife and open up to her so that she can know you. As Brother Lawrence says in *The Practice of the Presence of God*, "We must know before we can love" (Ninth Letter), and, "As knowledge is commonly the measure of love, the deeper and wider our knowledge, the greater will be our love" (Sixteenth Letter).

Wives: Respect involves giving your husband the benefit of the doubt, trusting him, cutting him some slack, and forgiving him. And none of this, "You're perfect, now change," stuff. The only way to change your husband is to change yourself.

Husbands: Remember that love is a verb—an action. The action can be small, such as a loving note where she will find it in the course of the day, but it should be clear enough to get the message across and for your wife to tell other women.

Wives: Remember that respect is conveyed by your tone of voice and your facial expression as well as your words.

When a husband shows love for his wife, she also feels respected; when a wife shows respect for her husband, he also feels loved.

Part Two
Proverbs from Elsewhere

A cheerful look makes a dish a feast.
—English Proverb[1]

This proverb gets at the heart of a successful marriage. A happy wife makes a husband feel loved and respected. A happy husband makes a wife feel safe and secure. Expressing your happiness—or at least contentment—will reassure your spouse. It's especially important to do this at mealtime.

You aren't always going to be happy when it's time to eat, of course, either because of the day's events or even because of your spouse. But if you put on a cheerful face and a kind, warm tone of voice, you'll not only make the dining experience more pleasant for those around you, but you might find that you are beginning to feel more cheerful, too.

And, if need be, after you enjoy the meal in peace and harmony, and allow your food and your thoughts to digest and settle, you can then discuss whatever issues need to be discussed— away from the table.

---

[1] George Herbert, *Outlandish Proverbs*. London: Humphrey Bluden, 1640. Proverb 62. Spelling modernized.

✠

Let all bitterness and wrath and anger and clamor and slander be put away from you, along with all malice. Be kind to one another, tender-hearted, forgiving each other, just as God in Christ also has forgiven you.
—Ephesians 4:31-32

A husband is not a project.
— American Proverb

Overheard in a restaurant: "He's really a nice guy. After we're married, there are only five things I want to change about him."

An attitude and expectation like this, of course, will result in a very stressful and unhappy marriage. Men do not want to be mothered (except when they are sick and their wives make lots of chicken soup for them). A man wants to feel competent and accepted. If he feels that his wife is trying to fix him, he will feel broken and rejected.

Wives and husbands should both understand that they can't change each other. Others have to want to change themselves. The only person you can change is yourself. But if you do change yourself, into a model that your spouse can treasure and enjoy, you'll soon discover that your spouse has chosen to change, too.

✝

Therefore if there is any encouragement in Christ, if there is any consolation of love, if there is any fellowship of the Spirit, if any affection and compassion, make my joy complete by being of the same mind, maintaining the

same love, united in spirit, intent on one purpose. Do nothing from selfishness or empty conceit, but with humility of mind regard one another as more important than yourselves; do not merely look out for your own personal interests, but also for the interests of others.
—*Philippians 2:1-4*

More have repented speech than silence.
--English Proverb[2]

Ever say something you regretted later? How many times? Ever regretted not saying something when you wanted to speak but didn't? How many times?

Seems as if some of us prove the proverb's accuracy. Mostly because some of us are blurters. We blurt out the first thing that comes to mind without first considering the impact or consequences on the receiver. And we blurt before listening long enough to understand the situation fully.

A good deal of repented speech comes from our bad interpersonal habits. One such habit is blaming. Instead of supporting their spouse by taking their spouse's side in an event, blamers habitually take the opposite side.

For example, one spouse comes home and says, "The boss chewed me out today for one tiny error on one spreadsheet."

The supportive spouse will say, "That's terrible. How can he be so critical when you work so hard?"

---

[2] Herbert, Proverb 682. Spelling modernized.

The blamer spouse will say, "Well, you ought to be more careful. Don't you check your work?"

You can see that in this situation, for the blamer (and for the sake of the blamer's spouse), silence would have been much better.

And now for another proverb about thinking before you speak:

> ✠ Once you throw a rock, you can't change your mind.

✞

Love is patient, love is kind and is not jealous; love does not brag and is not arrogant, does not act unbecomingly; it does not seek its own, is not provoked, does not take into account a wrong suffered, does not rejoice in unrighteousness, but rejoices with the truth; bears all things, believes all things, hopes all things, endures all things. Love never fails. . . .
—1 Corinthians 13:4-8a

A good husband makes a good wife.
A good wife makes a good husband.
　　　—English Proverbs[3]

You might have heard the parallel sayings, "Be glad about your husband's flaws, be- cause they are what kept him from getting a better wife," and "Be glad about your wife's flaws, because they are what kept her from get- ting a better husband."

The point is, instead of criticizing your spouse's shortcomings, model the kind of spouse you want your partner to be and be the kind of spouse your partner would enjoy and adore.

✚

Let all that you do be done in love.
　　　—1 Corinthians 16:14

---

[3] Wolfgang Mieder, ed., *The Prentice-Hall Encyclopedia of World Proverbs*. 1986. Rpt., New York: MJF Books, 1996. Proverbs 8224 and 17348.

When husband and wife agree with each other,
They can dry up the ocean with buckets.
—Vietnamese Proverb[4]

You've heard the expression that "two working together can do the work of three working by themselves." That's the benefit of teams.

This proverb reminds us that marriage is intended to be a collaboration, a joint effort, where the spouses form a team moving and working in the same direction, toward the same goals.

Spouses who play tug-of-war with each other are going to end up frustrated and tired, with little progress to show for the effort. If they would pull in the same direction, how much farther they could get.

Remember that you are a team with your spouse. Develop common goals and work together toward them. You are not two individuals who happen to be married; you are a collaborative team that should function as a unit.

---

[4] Mieder, Proverb 8241.

✟

Two are better than one because they have a good return for their labor. For if either of them falls, the one will lift up his companion. But woe to the one who falls when there is not another to lift him up. Furthermore, if two lie down together, they keep warm, but how can one keep warm alone? And if one can over-power him who is alone, two can resist him. A cord of three strands is not quickly torn apart.
—*Ecclesiastes 4:9-12*

Do not belittle the wife;
She is the home.
— African Proverb[5]

During the course of your marriage, you might live in a one-bedroom apartment, then a two or three bedroom apartment, then a condo or townhouse, then a starter-size single family house, and eventually a two-story house with a big yard.

But each one of these living structures will be your home at the time. What is it that makes a house into a home? Yes, it's your wife. As the proverb says, your wife *is* your home.

After a long trip, you are on the flight back. What do you tell the passenger next to you? "I'm on the way home to my house" or "I'm on the way home to my wife"?

You've heard the expression, "Home is where the heart is." When you are married, that means, "Home is where your wife is."

Cherish your home.

---

[5] Mieder, Proverb 17379.

✞

So husbands ought also to love their own wives as their own bodies. He who loves his own wife loves himself. . . .

—Ephesians 5:28

Men get the gist,
Women get the details.
— American Proverb

Men tend to remember the big picture, the general circumstances of an event, especially an interpersonal event (date, party, get together), while women remember the situation in detail.

Details that are important to a woman are often not important to a man. Note the following story, which I heard somewhere long ago.

Jim and Tim decided to go hunting one weekend. Jim stopped by Tim's house just long enough to pack Tim's gear into the pickup truck and wave goodbye to Tim's wife.

The two buddies had a great time, until about ten hours into their outing, they were separated while stalking a deer. When Jim didn't return to the campsite by the next morning, Tim took the truck back home and reported the incident. The authorities came to interview Tim.

"What was he wearing?" one officer asked.

"Normal hunting clothes," Tim said.

"Could you be more specific?" the officer said.

"Well, I'm not sure, but I think he had on a jacket." This was as detailed as Tim could be after spending ten hours with Jim.

On the other hand, Tim's wife, who had seen Jim for all of two minutes the day before, said, "He was wearing a red, black, and white plaid jacket, a brown shirt with button pockets, blue jeans with a black belt, and brown leather mid-calf lace-up boots."

Years later, when Tim told the story to others, he would say that Jim was wearing his camouflage jacket. His wife would correct him, making him upset.

When recounting events that they have remembered only the gist or summary of, men often fill in the details with plausible specifics, if they can't remember the actual details. (They may not realize they are doing this.)

In a marriage, these discrepancies can cause a lot of misunderstanding, disagreement, and criticism by the wife, since she remembers the details. To the husband the details don't matter, but are just window dressing. To hear his wife correct him over meaningless specifics makes him feel devalued and even insulted.

On the other hand, when specifics are important to a man, he will indeed recall the details. If we return to the story above, we will see just that.

"Was the man armed?" asked the officer.
"Yes, he had a gun," Tim's wife said.
"What kind?" the officer said.
"A rifle of some kind," she said.

"It was an Acme Model 8942 Conqueror .30 caliber modified bolt action rifle with an 8-power KillView scope," said Tim. "There was a slight scratch on the left side of the stock."

Tim's wife didn't care about the details of Jim's rifle and so didn't pay attention to them, just as Tim didn't care about the details of Jim's clothing.

Lessons for a happy marriage:

1. Wives, don't correct your husband in front of others, if at all. In casual conversation, the goal is not to establish every fact correctly; the goal is to be sociable.

2. Husbands, if you are in doubt about a social detail in your narrative (the date, location, and so forth), feel free to give a nod to your wife to fill in the blank. She will likely be glad to help you.

✠

. . . Walk in a manner worthy of the calling with which you have been called, with all humility and gentleness, with patience, showing forbearance to one another in love, being diligent to preserve the unity of the Spirit in the bond of peace.
—*Ephesians 4:1b-3*

Income, 100; outgo, 99; result: happiness.
Income, 100; outgo, 101; result: misery.
— After an English Proverb

What would a book about marriage be without a little financial advice?

These days, it seems, instead of trying to keep up with the Joneses (your neighbors, for those of you too young to recognize this cliché), folks are interested in keeping up with the movie stars or the rich and famous.

"There's the matching Jean Eric $7500 purse to go with my Roy Deekulus $3000 sweater, dear."

"And we could really use another giant screen TV for the bedroom, like the ones we have in the living room and family room. There's a great sale on now."

"Shall we just charge them, or do we need to take some more equity out of the house?"

The advice that you should live within your income is actually good advice. Pay your credit cards off every month. Save for major purchases and avoid having to pay interest.

It's one thing to argue—I mean have a discussion—about how to spend the money you have. It's quite another to argue about money you don't have. After all, Debt and Depression both start with the letter D. I'm just sayin'.

Bottom line: If you want to keep a smile on your spouse's face, restrain your spending, and match your outgo to your income, minus the 25% you should be saving and the 10% you should be tithing.

✦

"For which one of you, when he wants to build a tower, does not first sit down and calculate the cost to see if he has enough to complete it?"

—*Luke 14:28*

In marriage, expect less and enjoy more.
—Proverb

An unfortunate fact of life these days is that some people marry their own imaginations and neglect to understand the nature of the real person they married. After the wedding, a crisis occurs, where the spouse does not match—does not live up to—the expectations the other partner had imagined.

When each partner insists that the other change into the expected but imaginary person, more problems arise. (This situation is often referred to as "the big adjustment.")

The truth is that, if you want to be happy, reduce the expectations you have for your spouse and spend some time learning about whom you have actually married.

Another way to express this truth is that the degree of marital satisfaction can be measured by the distance between expectation and reality. The less the distance, the more the satisfaction.

Remember, too, that expectations are self-oriented—what you want—whereas a happy marriage is more likely to result from considering what you can give to the relationship.

Finally, it's one of those mysterious truths that once you eliminate or at least reduce your expectations (which often become demands), and once you start thinking about how you can serve the needs of your spouse, you'll be able to relax and go with the flow. And just when you don't expect it, happiness will ambush you.

✞

Now may the God of hope fill you with all joy and peace in believing, so that you will abound in hope by the power of the Holy Spirit.
—Romans 15:13

Marriage is a stack of lumber
And a keg of nails;
You have to build it yourself.
If the roof leaks, look to the carpenters.
—Proverb

Yes, the credit for a seamless, watertight marriage goes to God, working through the two carpenters who built it. But credit for the leaky roof goes to the couple alone, who didn't follow the directions very well. (Directions may be found in the Bible.)

If you partner with your spouse, if you put God first in your marriage, and if you agree on the pursuit of common goals, your roof won't leak.

Remember, when you are building together, you are making a sanctuary, not a coffin.

✢

But the fruit of the Spirit is love, joy, peace, patience, kindness, goodness, faithfulness, gentleness, self-control; against such things there is no law.
—Galatians 5:22-23

Small event, great meaning.
--Proverb

Marriage, like life itself, is about meaning, not experience. In a good marriage, the two spouses build meaning together. Meaning can be built around seemingly small events—a trip to the local coffee house, sharing a pack of gum, eating some tacos on the Tuesday special, reading something together, watching TV and eating popcorn. Or just talking.

When love is active, meaning is everywhere. Don't think you need to fly to a fancy resort halfway across the globe, tightrope walk together across the Grand Canyon, or run down the streets of Pamplona just ahead of 2,000 bulls. You need none of these things to share the deepest meanings. Love adds to the meaning of even the smallest experience. Love creates its own meaning.

So, if you're on a severe budget, don't grind up your soul with regret and envy of the rich. You have each other.

✦

"For this reason I say to you, do not be worried about your life, as to what you will eat or what you will drink; nor for your body, as to what you will put on. Is not life more than food, and the body more than clothing? Look at the birds of the air, that they do not sow, nor reap nor gather into barns, and yet your heavenly Father feeds them. Are you not worth much more than they?

And who of you by being worried can add a single hour to his life? And why are you worried about clothing? Observe how the lilies of the field grow; they do not toil nor do they spin, yet I say to you that not even Solomon in all his glory clothed himself like one of these. But if God so clothes the grass of the field, which is alive today and tomorrow is thrown into the furnace, will He not much more clothe you? You of little faith!

Do not worry then, saying, 'What will we eat?' or 'What will we drink?' or 'What will we wear for clothing?' For the Gentiles eagerly seek all these things; for your heavenly Father knows that you need all these things. But seek first His kingdom and His righteousness, and all these things will be added to you. So do not worry about tomorrow; for tomorrow will care for itself. Each day has enough trouble of its own."

—Matthew 6:25-34

In marriage, the journey is the destination.
—Proverb

Marriage, like success, is often misdefined. Some say, wrongly, that success means finally achieving an ultimate goal—of fame, wealth, or power. Actually, success is better defined as making progress toward a worthy goal. Thus, you can be successful over a long period, as long as you are making progress.

Similarly, marriage is often wrongly thought of as "the main chance," the final stage of a relationship, the ultimate goal of perpetual happiness reached at last.

But marriage is not a destination to reach and rest. Nor is it the first step in an ultimate destination (kids? old age? death?). Marriage is a journey you take with your best friend, through many adventures, happy and otherwise. Marriage is a long-term creative problem-solving activity, a trip through many physical and emotional landscapes, a flight of two souls up and down the spiritual ladder from heaven to—well, you get the idea.

Apologies to you realists for my waxing so lyrical, but I wanted to make and rub in the point that marriage is a collection of events, some terminal and some ongoing, some major and most not.

You have probably heard the saying, "Life is what happens while you're making other plans." And since marriage is now a part of your life, its events will happen whether you plan them or not.

Okay, the point is, enjoy the ride. Certainly you want to plan and work toward major milestones. But it's crucial also to explore—and enjoy—your marriage relationship not just in the big goals, like that vacation to Europe, but in the minor events of everyday living:

"John, the dog barfed on the living room carpet again. Can you bring the pet odor killer?"
"Sure, honey. Need anything else?"
"A couple more rags."
"You got 'em."
"I love you."

You might have heard the saying, "Getting there is half the fun." Double that and you have a marriage. When the ride is smooth, you can embrace sweetly. When you hit the potholes, hold on to each other all the more tightly.

✞

Let love be without hypocrisy. Abhor what is evil; cling to what is good. Be devoted to one another in brotherly love; give preference to one another in honor; not lagging behind in diligence, fervent in spirit, serving the Lord;

rejoicing in hope, persevering in tribulation, devoted to prayer. . . .
—*Romans 12:9-12*

Marriage math doesn't add up.
—Proverb

Marriage is not a transactional relationship, where spouses exchange one thing or service for another, always making sure they don't get swindled. Marriage is an all-in relationship, where each spouse strives to serve and help the other, without keeping score.

But what does it mean to say that marriage math doesn't add up? Let's look at a couple of examples.

Before they got married, Mike did a certain amount of house cleaning each week. Let's call it 2 housekeeping units (2 HKUs). His soon-to-be bride, Lisa, did three times as much, or 6 HKUs. (That's pretty typical—women are generally much neater than men.)

So, after they get married, both Mike and Lisa are thinking they will be sharing housekeeping tasks (Mike is such a good guy), and they both think this means having to do only half as much work as before, with their loving spouse doing the other half.

Okay, so they get married. Now, let's do the math. Mike reduces his work to 1 HKU per week. Lisa reduces her work to 3 HKUs per week. Mike thinks everything is fine, as both have reduced their housekeeping by half. But to Lisa, Mike is doing only one third of what she expected him to do. She thinks that when she reduced her work by 3 HKUs, Mike would do the other 3. Tension results. Maybe even conflict.

In the example above, Lisa probably thinks Mike should conform to her model of housekeeping. But that would mean that, while she enjoys cutting her housekeeping work by half, Mike would have to increase his work by half. Marriage math just doesn't add up.

Here's another example of marriage math gone wrong:

Sandy: I realize that marriage is a give-and-take relationship. So, when I get married, I expect to give fifty percent and get fifty percent.

Sandy is in for a rude awakening, because she is a scorekeeper—someone who plans to keep track of who does what, and to make sure that everything in the marriage is "fair." But scorekeepers, without realizing their bias toward themselves, tend to add 25 points to their side while subtracting 25 points from their spouse's side.

In fact, marriage math is so wacky that, for Sandy's determination to give 50 percent and take 50 percent, while her spouse will do the same, she will find that 50 plus 50 equals 25. And that's why, even if both spouses pledge to make a 100 percent effort, the scorekeeper isn't going to be happy.

Advice: Don't keep score. The numbers just don't add up. Instead, give and serve, give and serve. Or as it's sometimes put, "See a job, do a job."

✤

Do all things without grumbling or disputing; so that you will prove yourselves to be blameless and innocent, children of God above reproach in the midst of a crooked and perverse generation, among whom you appear as lights in the world. . . .
                    —Philippians 2:14-15

Once forgiven, twice forgotten.
—Proverb

This proverb serves to remind us that once we forgive a spouse for some wrongdoing, that wrongdoing must never be mentioned again, especially in the context of a dispute.

During an argument, some spouses have a tendency to bring up every past wrong they can remember, as a form of additional ammunition.

However, bringing up a past wrong has no relevance to the current situation. It's only purpose is to inflict emotional harm on the spouse.

Moreover, to remember a transgression from the past and to bring it up again during an argument means that it was never really forgiven before. Instead, it has been harbored and nurtured and held as a grudge, waiting to be flung in the face of the wrongdoer during the next disagreement.

If you sincerely forgive a wrong, put it from your mind; forget it. Then, if during an argument, the wrong comes to mind again, forget it again. Do not mention it. It's a dead issue.

✝

"For if you forgive others for their transgressions, your heavenly Father will also forgive you. But if you do not forgive others, then your Father will not forgive your transgressions."
—*Matthew 6:14-15*

If married love and joy come to an end,
To blame your mate is spitting in the wind.
—Proverb

Let's just assume that, if there is sand in the machinery of your marriage, you were both at the beach earlier; so it's better to work together to clean out the grit than to try to figure out just whose sand it is.

I know, I know, it's not you. It's all your partner's problem. But here's a thought: If your marriage is troubled, *pray that it's all your fault.*

Huh? Well, look at it this way. The only person you can change is you. So, if the unhappiness and frustration in the marriage are on your side, there's hope! You can change! Your marriage can get better!

Remember, you can't change your spouse—except by modeling the Golden Proverb[6] to such an extent that your spouse will choose to change out of love and gratitude.

---

[6] On page 76.

✠

"Why do you look at the speck that is in your brother's eye, but do not notice the log that is in your own eye? Or how can you say to your brother, 'Let me take the speck out of your eye,' and behold, the log is in your own eye? You hypocrite, first take the log out of your own eye, and then you will see clearly to take the speck out of your brother's eye."
—Matthew 7:3-5

Be to your spouse
What you want your spouse
To be to you.
— The Golden Proverb

Say this out loud: "If I am critical, disrespect-ful, controlling, negative, cold, rejecting, and resentful toward my spouse, my spouse will become warm, affectionate, loving, kind, and happy." How does that sound? Not very plau-sible? So then, why do some spouses behave as if they believe this?

Now say this out loud: "If I am warm, affec-tionate, loving, kind, and happy with my spouse, my spouse will be the same with me." Does that seem to be at least a little more likely?

The original Golden Rule, of course, was meant to be a rule of personal moral behavior, not a method for creating reciprocal behavior. But in marriage, the Golden Proverb does, in fact, work. And it works both ways: Spouses tend to treat each other the way they are treat-ed.

✟

Finally, brethren, whatever is true, whatever is honorable, whatever is right, whatever is pure, whatever is lovely, whatever is of good repute, if there is any excellence and if anything worthy of praise, dwell on these things.
—Philippians 4:8

Maturity can be measured
By the size of what upsets you.
—Proverb

Some people become furious when there is a small piece of gristle in the steak, when the toilet paper roll isn't replaced, or when a dish is left in the sink instead of being put in the dishwasher. If one spouse paid fifty cents more for the same item that was on sale for less elsewhere, the other spouse thinks a hateful, demeaning attack is justified.

And then there are those spouses who ignore, tolerate, or forgive not only small irregularities like those above, but also substantial mistakes. Call this maturity, or love, or understanding—or perspective.

Speaking of perspective, here is a little story that might help you understand that in the overall context of life and marriage, little differences from what you prefer are really not so important after all.

Mrs. Jones walked sternly into the living room and glared at Mr. Jones. "You left the cap off the toothpaste tube again," she said harshly. "Why can't you ever remember to put it back on? It's not that hard. Even a child can do it."

"And why can't you ever remember to turn off the coffee pot?" retorted Mr. Jones. *"It was still on when I got home this evening. I swear, one day you're going to burn the house down."*

"Maybe I'd remember to turn off the coffee pot if I wasn't so distracted by having to pick up your dirty socks and underwear, which you leave all over the house. You know, there is a hamper to put your dirty clothes in, right next to that big white box called a washing machine. Do you want me to show you where it is?"

"Speaking of washing, I noticed the other day that you use way too much shampoo. And you buy that expensive salon junk which isn't any better than the cheap brand."

Just as Mrs. Jones was about to deliver a snarling response to Mr. Jones, as they both were gearing up for another heated, three-hour argument, the phone rang. Mr. Jones moved his glare from his wife to the phone as he answered it: *"Yeah, what is it?"*

"Hello. This is Officer Clayton Smith. Is Mr. John Jones available"?

"This is John Jones. What do you want?" Mr. Jones demanded.

"Mr. Jones, do you have a daughter named Jennifer Nicole Jones?"

"Yes, yes," answered Mr. Jones, testily. *"What has she done this time?"*

"I'm sorry," said Officer Smith, *"but your daughter was in an automobile accident this evening. The driver lost control and crashed. Your daughter was trapped inside when the car exploded in flames."*

✝

So, as those who have been chosen of God, holy and beloved, put on a heart of compassion, kindness, humility, gentleness and patience; bearing with one another, and forgiving each other, whoever has a complaint against any-one; just as the Lord forgave you, so also should you. Beyond all these things put on love, which is the perfect bond of unity. Let the peace of Christ rule in your hearts, to which indeed you were called in one body; and be thankful.
—Colossians 3:12-15

Your husband is not your father
That you should punish him,
Nor your brother that you should rival him.
Your wife is not your mother
That you should take her for granted,
Nor your sister
That you should compete with her.
— Proverb

This proverb is a reminder to check your emotional baggage to see if you have unresolved issues with a parent or sibling that you might unknowingly transfer onto your spouse.

This transfer seems to occur with some frequency, so it needed to be mentioned. It's unjust to get revenge on your father by punishing your husband or to even the score with your sister by treating your wife as a competitor or an enemy.

✚

"For this reason a man shall leave his father and mother, and the two shall become one flesh; so they are no longer two, but one flesh."
—Mark 10:7-8

To find your marriage, lose yourself.
— Proverb

Even casual observation of happily married couples reveals that the key to a warm and loving relationship is that both spouses have learned to get themselves — their egos — off the throne of their hearts, put Jesus on the throne, and become humble servants of each other. By contrast, unhappily married couples have super-glued themselves to their own thrones.

The problem is pride. Pride equals me, self, selfish, my way, my standards, my needs, my decisions, my power, my control. Pride is judgmental, critical, demanding, scorekeeping, contentious.

Humility is a focus on others. It is selfless, accepting, grateful, serving, giving, thoughtful, deferential.

It's just a bit of a challenge to get close to or feel loving toward a dictator who acts as if you just don't measure up. A good marriage features the embrace of souls, a comfortable, warm hearted twining of affection. In order to have this, you and your spouse must both yield — you must lose yourself — and team up to work as one.

Instead of thinking about "me, my, and mine," think about what you can do to fulfill your spouse's needs and wants, how you can give of yourself instead of taking for yourself, what you can do for the team. You'll get a lot more satisfaction—and even happiness—than you will from a prideful obsession with yourself.

✝

And all of you, clothe yourselves with humility toward one another, for God is opposed to the proud, but gives grace to the humble.
—1 Peter 5:5

Criticizing your spouse for an accident
Pours salt into an open wound.
—Proverb

Suppose your spouse drops grandma's favorite gravy bowl, or knocks over the iced tea glass in a restaurant when you are out to dinner together. What is your reaction? Do you get angry and say something like, "Why can't you be more careful?" or "That was grandma's pride and joy and now it's ruined forever. What's wrong with you? Must you be so clumsy?"

Let's think about this. The definition of an accident is an unfortunate event occurring without intent. The person responsible (1) didn't want it to happen and (2) feels unhappy that it did happen and (3) needs comfort and reassurance that the misadventure is survivable.

Therefore, responding with angry criticism not only deprives your spouse of the support and compassion he or she needs, but it compounds the feelings of guilt, sorrow, and regret without adding a grain of sand toward repairing the loss. Worse, it telegraphs to your spouse that you cannot be relied on to offer aid in times of emotional distress: You won't be the go-to person when your spouse is facing the stressors and failures we all encounter.

Here's a story drawn from real life.

I opened the cupboard where the spices are kept and a glass pepper grinder fell out onto the floor and shattered, throwing glass and peppercorns all over the kitchen. When my wife got home, we had a choice of three ways to interact about this event.

(1) My wife could blame the accident on me. *"Oh, that was my only pepper grinder, and my only whole peppercorns. How could you have been so careless? You just don't care about my things, do you? And now I'll have to wear shoes in the kitchen to avoid stepping on broken glass, because the way you clean up, there will still be shards all over the place. And the poor dog will probably cut his feet and then get blood all over the carpet. I hope you're happy."*

(2) I could blame the accident on my wife. *"When I opened the cupboard, the pepper grinder fell out and shattered all over the place. Now I have to clean it up. You must have carelessly put it in an unsafe position. I could have been cut by the glass when it fell out. Why can't you be more careful when you put things away?"*

(3) What really happened.
Me: "We've had an accident. When I opened the cupboard, the pepper grinder fell out on the floor and broke. I need to clean it up before we can eat dinner."
My wife: "How can I help you clean it up?"
Me: "Where's a broom?"

My wife: "I'll get it. What else do you need?"
Me: "Maybe the vacuum."
My wife: "I'll sweep it up."
Me: "No, I'll do it. You relax."

Quiz Time: (1) Which of the three scenarios would you have chosen, and what would the resulting interaction have been like? (2) How would your chosen scenario have impacted your relationship with your spouse? (3) Would that impact be worth it?

✞

So then we pursue the things which make for peace and the building up of one another.
—Romans 14:19

Anger brings loss.
[Hasira, hasara.]
—Swahili proverb

Remember this two-word Swahili proverb (which literally means "anger, loss" or "anger, damage") next time you are tempted to lash out at your spouse, who is or ought to be your best friend and the love of your life.

Enough said.

✞

Do not let the sun go down on your anger.
—Ephesians 4:26b

A cheerful wife is the spice of life.
— French proverb

As has been said by many observers, men are simple creatures when it comes to relationships with women. Men want their wives to offer them respect, affirmation, and encouragement. A husband interprets a cheerful, happy wife as embodying all these things, making him feel as if he is doing well. And he is motivated to do things to keep her happy.

If his wife is not cheerful, if there always seems to be something wrong — especially if it's something wrong with him — the husband feels that he doesn't measure up and becomes discouraged. Unhappiness, drama, and discontent in a wife put enormous stress on husbands, who often try not to show it. But the proverb is true — no, it's understated: A cheerful wife is her husband's delight.

✠

Is anyone cheerful? He is to sing praises.
— *James 5:13b*

Marriage is a dance.
—Proverb

This concluding proverb reminds us of the key truths about marriage. This is truly marriage in a nutshell:

1. Someone has to lead. In a Biblical, Christian marriage, this is the husband. (Thinking that "When we disagree, we'll just compromise," doesn't always work.) Let your husband lead and you might be surprised how often he defers to his wife.

2. The two partners must learn to move together as one unit. Unless you dance as one, your movement will be called "stepping on feet," or "falling down" rather than "dancing."

3. Practice over time improves your skill. As a friend once said about her own marriage, "It gets better."

4. The most beautiful dances require that you keep each other close and hold on.

5. The meaning of the dance is something beyond either partner individually. (It's about the dance, not about you.)

6. The more the combined and focused energy, the more amazing the dance.

7. Two people dancing together is a lot more fun than one person trying to dance alone.

✞

Marriage is to be held in honor among all. . . .
—Hebrews 13:4a

Appendix 1
The Choice

The table below contains many of the words found in both the Biblical proverbs and the proverbs from other sources. As you read them over, think about your relationship with your spouse and then compare your behavior with the descriptions in the table below.

How to Make And How to Be A Happy Spouse	How to Make And How to Be An Unhappy Spouse
compassionate	critical
kind	contradicting
humble	angry
gentle	negative
patient	unloving
forgiving	shaming
loving	selfish
supporting	combative
partnering	competitive
appreciative	argumentative
thankful	whining
sympathetic	blaming
faithful	gruff
serving	demanding
pleasant	rejecting

How to Make And How to Be A Happy Spouse	How to Make And How to Be An Unhappy Spouse
amiable	dominating
gracious	controlling
giving	distrusting
positive	contemptuous
complimenting	cold
uplifting	thoughtless
cheerful	insulting
thoughtful	sulking
generous	haughty
affirming	negating
listening	lecturing

You can draw your own conclusions from the results. If you don't like what you realize, you know exactly what to do.

✢

See that no one repays another with evil for evil, but always seek after that which is good for one another and for all people.
—1 Thessalonians 5:15

Appendix 2
The Magic Words

Saying the magic words regularly (daily for some of them) can help keep your marriage healthy and happy. Try it. They really work.

I love you
Thank you
You are right
Forgive me
You're smart
I'm sorry
Please
I agree completely
You're beautiful
I was wrong
You have my support
I forgive you
I'm glad I married you

About the Editor and Commentator

Robert Harris was born in 1950 in Los Angeles, California. He holds a PhD in English from the University of California at Riverside.

His interest in marriage and relationships started many years ago, while he was still single, observing married couples interact. He saw some couples function as a harmonious unit and other couples treating each other as enemies. In later years, continued observation, personal experience, and substantial research led him to consider sharing what he had learned. He began mounting Web pages about improving relationships.

Then one day he witnessed a young couple in a supermarket arguing in hostile tones over whether to buy a particular jar of jelly. It occurred to him then that a short, easily accessible little book about marriage might be helpful for such couples. Not long after that, he was reading in the book of Proverbs, and the idea for the current volume took root.

Dr. Harris lives in Tustin with his excellent wife, Marie.

Scripture Index

Colophon
Proverbs set in *Monotype Corsiva 14*
Comments set in Book Antiqua 11
Scripture passages set in *Georgia 11 italic*